SHRIGLEY HAVE SEX IN YOUR BEER

BY

DAVID ANTS

SYMPATHY

ANGER   THE WRA~ ~F GOD

IDEAS

REDSTONE

D0808176

First published 2007

Redstone Press
7a St Lawrence Terrace, London W10 5SU
www.redstonepress.co.uk

Layout: Kim McKinney
Artwork: Otis Marchbank
Production: Tim Chester
Printed in China by C & C Offset Printing

ISBN 978-1-870003-54-4

A CIP record for this book is available from the British Library

 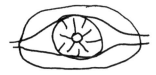

CHAPTER ONE

IT IS A JOKE

IT IS NOT A JOKE

IT IS A JOKE

IT IS NOT A JOKE

IT IS A JOKE

IT IS NOT A JOKE

IT IS A JOKE

IT IS NOT A JOKE

IT IS A JOKE

IT IS NOT A JOKE

IT IS A JOKE

IT IS NOT A JOKE

IT IS A JOKE

IT IS NOT A JOKE

IT IS A JOKE

IT IS NOT A JOKE

IT IS A JOKE

IT IS NOT A JOKE

IT IS A JOKE

IT IS NOT A JOKE

THE IDEA

WHEN I FIRST HAD THE IDEA I WAS WORRIED. I THOUGHT IT WAS A SIGN THAT I WAS GOING MAD.

BUT THEN I SAW A PROGRAMME ON TELEVISION ABOUT IT AND I REALISED THAT A GREAT MANY PEOPLE HAD THE SAME IDEA AND THAT IT IS NOT ▬ MADNESS AT ALL, IT IS PERFECTLY NORMAL. I HAVE NOW COME TO THINK THAT THE MAD PEOPLE ARE THE ONES WHO HAVE NOT HAD THIS IDEA, IN FACT I HAVE BECOME VERY WORRIED ABOUT IT.

I LIKE IT WHEN
YOU SPEAK TO ME IN A
HIGH-PITCHED VOICE

I LIKE IT WHEN
YOU SAY THINGS LIKE
'LET'S PRETEND WE'RE
IN A TUNNEL'

I LIKE IT WHEN
YOU SUGGEST WE
CRAWL

I LIKE IT WHEN
YOU EXTINGUISH
THE LIGHTS

I DO NOT LIKE IT WHEN
YOU BITE ME

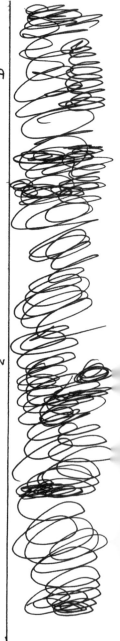

I AM GOING TO TELL YOU ~~BLESOME~~
SOME THINGS:

THE GRASS IS BLUE

THE SKY IS GREEN

THE SEA IS RED

THE SUN COMES OUT AT NIGHT

EAST IS WEST

WHAT GOES UP DOES NOT NECESSARILY
HAVE TO COME DOWN

A ROLLING STONE GATHERS MOSS AS IT
IS ROLLING. EVENTUALLY THE MOSS
BUILDS UP TO SUCH AN EXTENT THAT
THE STONE IS NO LONGER ABLE TO
ROLL (THIS CAN HAPPEN IN JUST A
FEW DAYS)

ONLY DADDY CAN USE THE
BARBEQUE

I AM NOT ALLOWED TO USE
THE BARBEQUE

I WILL BE PUNISHED IF I
USE THE BARBEQUE

DEAR SIR

I KNOW THAT
YOU ARE ~~XX~~ EXCESSIVELY PROUD
OF YOUR APPEARACE
AND THAT YOU HAVE ~~XXX~~ HAD SOME
JUSTIFICATION FOR YOUR PRIDE

BUT I FEEL THAT I
MUST IMPART AN AWFUL
TRUTH TO YOU
ONE THAT WILL NOT BE KIND

THE FACT IS
THAT YOUR LOOKS
HAVE FADED AND
NOW YOU ARE
NO MORE HANDSOME

THAN ~~X~~
A
BAKED
POTATO

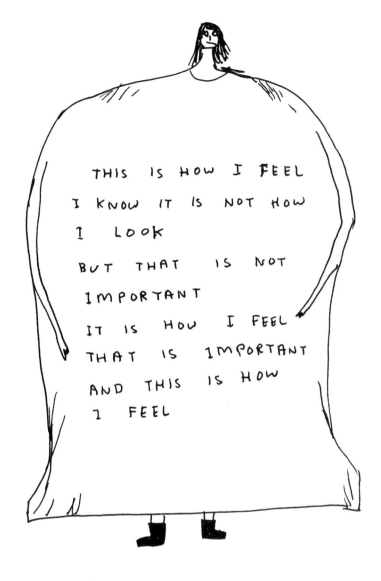

MEOW
(GIVE ME FOOD)
MEOW
(IF YOU DIED I WOULD NOT CARE)
MEOW
(I WOULD GO AND LIVE NEXT DOOR)
MEOW
(YOU ARE A STUPID OLD WOMAN)

MUCH AS I LIKE YOU

I ~~AM~~ AM OBLIGED TO HURT YOU

FOR I AM A TORTURER

AND YOU ARE IN POSSESSION

OF INFORMATION

THAT I MUST EXTRACT

IF YOU TELL ME WHAT

I WANT TO KNOW

BEFORE I BEGIN

I WILL STILL HAVE TO TORTURE YOU

FOR A WHILE

IT IS JUST THE WAY

THAT THESE THINGS ARE DONE

SORRY

FEELINGS

FEELINGS
NOTHING MORE THAN FEELINGS
TRYING TO FORGET ABOUT
THE RECENT SPATE OF KILLINGS

EAR RINGS
NOTHING MORE THAN EAR RINGS
TRY NOT TO GET ANGRY
BECAUSE YOU'VE LOST YOUR EAR RINGS

PREACHER IS OUTSIDE THE CHURCH STEPS
CLEANING BLOOD FROM THE
EARLIER HIS CONGREGATION BEAT
A MAN SENSELESS FOR BEING
A NON-BELIEVER.

I HOPE I NEVER LOSE MY FAITH.

THINKS THE PREACHER.

AND IF I DO
I HOPE THE CONGREGATION
DON'T FIND OUT ABOUT IT.

THIS DAY
WAS MUCH LIKE OTHER DAYS
EXCEPT THAT
THERE WAS
A HUGE EXPLOSION
AND MANY PEOPLE WERE KILLED

YESTERDAY
WAS MUCH LIKE OTHER DAYS
EXCEPT THAT
UNKNOWN TO MOST
A HUGE BOMB WAS PLANTED
IN THE CENTRE OF TOWN

TOMORROW
WILL BE MUCH THE SAME
AS THE LATTER PART
OF TODAY
I.E.:
CLEARING UP BODIES,
CARING FOR THE WOUNDED, ETC.

I LOOKED UP AND SAW

A ROBOT AT THE WINDOW
OF THE FACTORY
THERE WAS A SIGN
ON THE DOOR
THAT SAID
'WORKERS NOT REQUIRED AT PRESENT
SO I WENT HOME

- - - - - - - - - - - - - - - - - - - -

WRITING IN MY DIARY

WHO'S BEEN WRITING IN MY DIARY?
WRITING ABOUT THINGS I HAVEN'T DONE
AND THOUGHTS I HAVEN'T ~~HAVE~~ HAD?
~~~~ SAYING THAT I LOVE PEOPLE
WHO I DON'T LOVE?
~~~~ AND THAT I HATE PEOPLE
WHO I DON'T HATE?
AND HOW ~~~~ WERE THEY
ABLE TO COPY MY HANDWRITING
SO ~~~~ ACCURATELY?

HOORAY FOR THIS PICTURE
HOORAY FOR HE WHO DREW IT
DAMN THOSE WHO WILL NOT
PARTICIPATE IN THE CHEERING

SIZE OF A PEA
SHAPE OF A PEA
COLOUR OF A PEA
IMPORTANCE OF PEA
PEA GIVEN AS A GIFT
PEA GIVEN AS A PRIZE
PEA GIVEN TO CHILD AS A TOY
PEA CONFISCATED AS PUNISHMENT

THIS IS WHERE I KEEP MY BONES

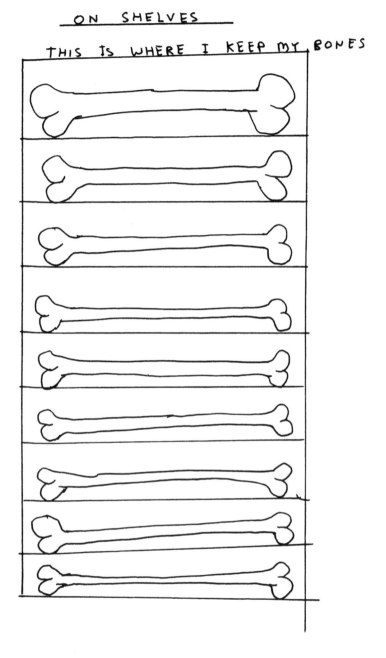

IT'S GETTING DARK

WINGS

THE POPULAR GROUP FEATURING
PAUL McCARTNEY AND HIS WIFE.
THE ~~GROUP~~ GROUP NO LONGER EXISTS,
SHE IS DEAD, HE IS OLD.
IT IS A SHAME.

THE ANGEL HAS
ARRIVED

HE IS NOT
AS WE
EXPECTED

UPON MY ~~GOOSE~~ RETURN FROM EXILE
I ENTER THE TOWN
RIDING A GIANT GOOSE

THE GOOSE
WILL PECK THE
FUCK OUT OF
ANY PROTESTORS

WHAT DO YOU FEEL?

I FEEL NOTHING

WHAT DO YOU SEE?

I SEE NOTHING, OR
AT LEAST, NOTHING I
CARE FOR

WHAT DO YOU WANT?

I WANT A MASSAGE

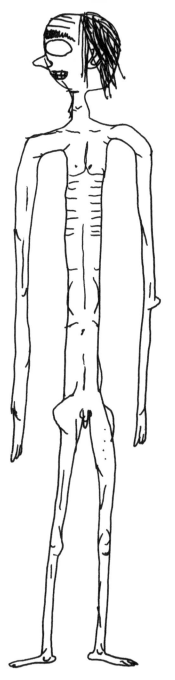

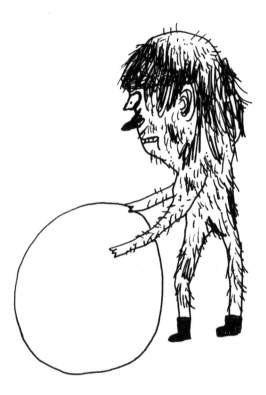

HOW COME HE GETS TO
PLAY WITH THE BALL?
HE SHOULDN'T BE ALLOWED
TO PLAY WITH THE BALL.
I WANT TO PLAY WITH THE BALL

LIVING IN A DRAIN

IT'S NO FUN LIVING IN A DRAIN

IT'S FUN IF YOU'RE A RAT

PROBABLY

BUT IT'S NO FUN IF YOU'RE A MAN

HIDING FROM THE POLICE

PLEASE

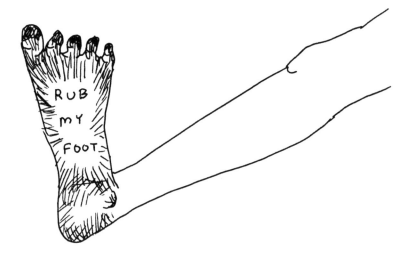

I WILL GIVE YOU
TEN EUROS NOW AND
TWENTY EUROS AFTERWARDS

AS I WENT TO PICK UP
THE KNIFE I SAW MY REFLECTION
IN THE BLADE. I DECIDED TO
GO TO THE BATHROOM TO
COMB MY HAIR. WHILE
I WAS COMBING MY HAIR
MY CAPTIVES ESCAPED.
DAMN! DAMN! DAMN!
NEVER MIND.

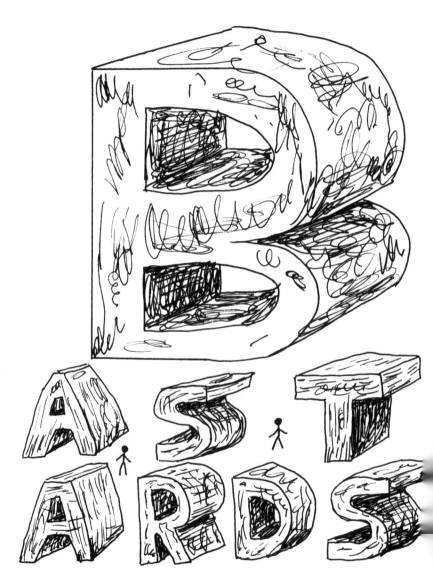

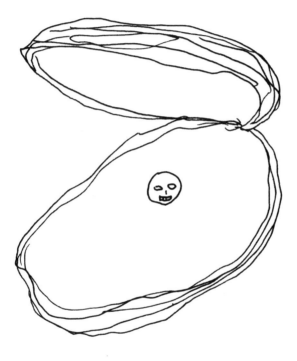

I'M SPECIAL

ANTENNA

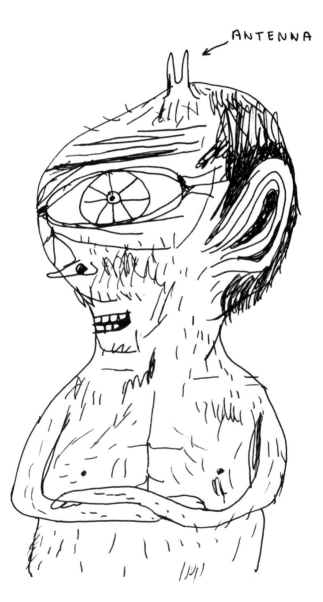

MY HELL

YOU ARE NOT ALLOWED
IN MY HELL
YOU MUST STAY IN
YOUR OWN HELL

THANK - YOU
THANK - YOU
THANK - YOU
THANK - YOU
THANK - YOU
THANK - YOU
THANK - YOU
THANK - YOU
THANK - YOU
THANK - YOU
THANK - YOU
THANK - YOU
THANK - YOU

STOP   IT
STOP   IT
STOP   IT
STOP   IT
STOP   IT

THANKS AGAIN
_____

YOU MUST LEAVE NOW

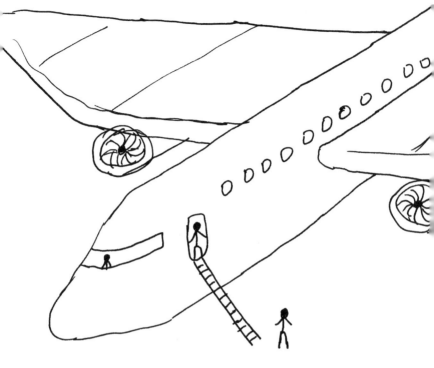

YOU ARE WELCOME ONBOARD
AS LONG AS YOU DO NOT ~~mess~~
MESS ABOUT
AN AIRCRAFT IS NO PLACE
FOR SILLY GAMES

I DREW THIS

I MEANT NOTHING BY IT

BUT THEY PUT ME IN JAIL

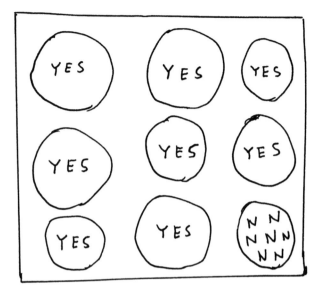

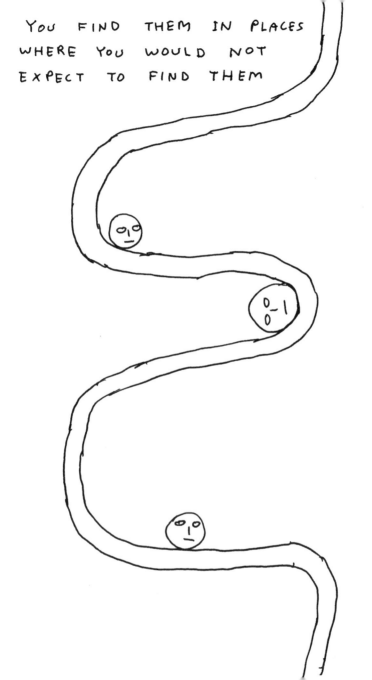

YOU FIND THEM IN PLACES
WHERE YOU WOULD NOT
EXPECT TO FIND THEM

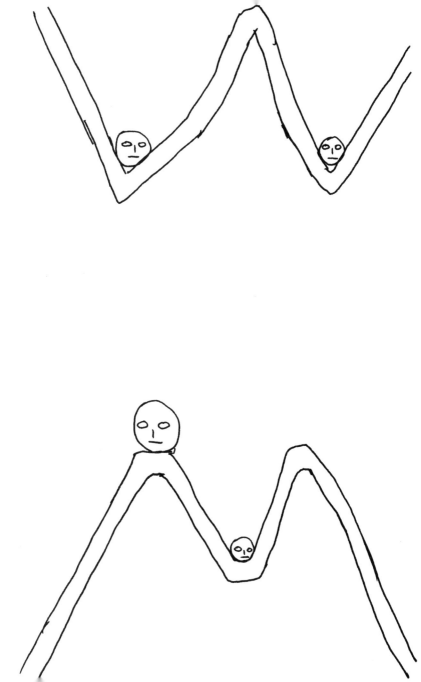

HOW CAN I BE A BETTER MAN?

PERHAPS I SHOULD TAKE A WIFE
AND SIRE SOME CHILDREN
NO!
I SHALL BECOME A MONK
AND DEVOTE
MYSELF TO
GOD

LOSING YOUR WAY

IF YOU FEEL YOU ARE LOSING
YOUR WAY
DON'T BE AFRAID TO ASK
DIRECTIONS
I LOST MY WAY
AND I DIDN'T ASK DIRECTIONS
AND LOOK WHERE IT GOT ME

I HAVE SAMPLED THE VOICE
OF CHARLES MANSON
AND I HAVE USED IT TO MAKE
A DANCE RECORD

THE RECORD IS GOOD AND
I AM VERY PROUD OF IT

MY NAME

DAVID !
DAVID !
DAVID !
DAVID !
DAVID !
DAVID !
DAVID !
DAVID !
DAVID !
DAVID !
DAVID !
DAVID !
DAVID !
DAVID !
OH DO PLEASE STOP SHOUTING
MY NAME

I WAS IN HER
BAG
SHE CARRIED ME
AMONGST HER
THINGS
IT WAS JOY

I WISH I HAD MY OWN THINGS

I WISH I HAD MY OWN THINGS
IF I HAD MY OWN THINGS
I WOULDN'T HAVE TO STEAL YOURS

I WISH I HAD MY OWN GIRLFRIEND
FOR THE SAME REASON

I WISH I HAD MY OWN THOUGHTS
FOR THE SAME REASON

A CALL TO ARMS

I CHALLENGE THEE ALL
TO COME TO MY AID
I AM DROWNING IN A SEA OF TROUBLE
ALL MY FOES SURROUND ME
AND
THOUGH I AM NOT ENTIRELY DESERWING
OF RESCUE
I WOULD LIKE YOU ALL TO HELP ME
PLEASE

HER FACE
POPS UP
UNEXPECTEDLY
ALL THE TIME
IN MAGAZINES
ON TELEVISION
AND
IN MY MIND
AND
ON MONEY
SHE IS OUR QUEEN

PANDERING TO POPULAR OPINION

YOU HAVE BEEN FOUND GUILTY OF
PANDERING TO POPULAR OPINION
HOW DO YOU PLEAD ?
NOT GUILTY ?
THEN YOU WILL FACE A TRIAL
IN THE COURT OF POPULAR OPINION
IF THEY FIND YOU INNOCENT
IT MEANS YOU ARE GUILTY

CROSSINGS OUT

WHY ARE ▪ THERE SO MANY
CROSSINGS OUT ?
IS THERE SOME ▬▬▬ MEANING
BEHIND IT ?
I DEMAND TO ▬▬ KNOW

WE LIVE IN A BEAUTIFUL WORLD
BUT THE WORLD CAN EASILY
BE SPOILED
I FEAR THAT I HAVE
ACCIDENTALLY SPOILED THE WORLD
AND I AM VERY SORRY
I AM VERY SORRY INDEED
I AM SO VERY CLUMSY YOU SEE

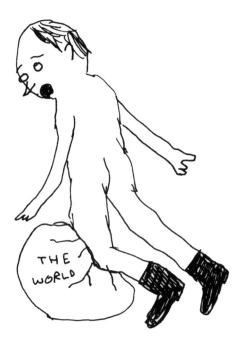

BAD WEATHER

I AM EXTREMELY HAPPY DESPITE THE BAD WEATHER

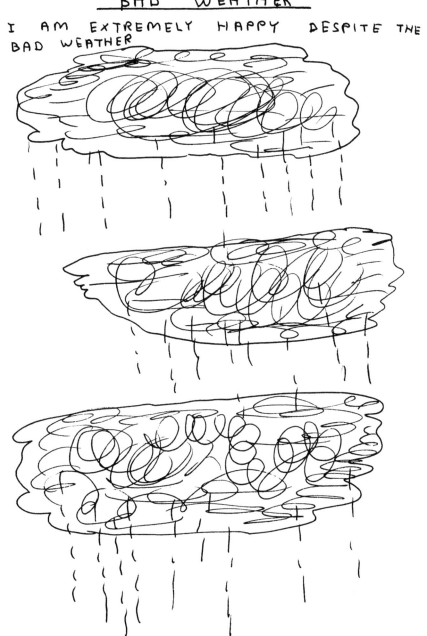

HUMPTY DUMPTY
SAT ON A WALL
HUMPTY DUMPTY
HAD GREAT FALL
HUMPTY DUMPTY
HAD A SEIZURE
AND SWALLOWED HIS TONGUE

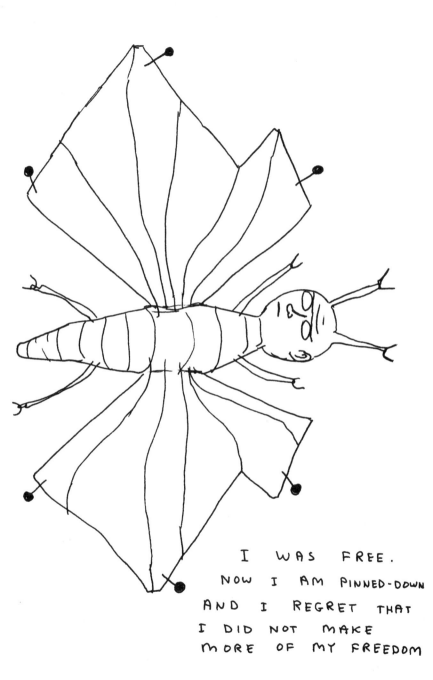

I WAS FREE.
NOW I AM PINNED-DOWN
AND I REGRET THAT
I DID NOT MAKE
MORE OF MY FREEDOM

THE THOUGHTS OF A SHEEP

THE SHEEP-SHEARER HAS ARRIVED
BUT I WILL NOT LET HIM SHEAR ME
I DO NOT CONSIDER IT APPROPRIATE
FOR HIM TO SHEAR ME
HE IS A VULGAR MAN
WITH TATTOOS UP HIS ARMS
I WOULD RATHER DIE
AND BE EATEN
THAN LET HIM
HAVE MY PRECIOUS WOOL

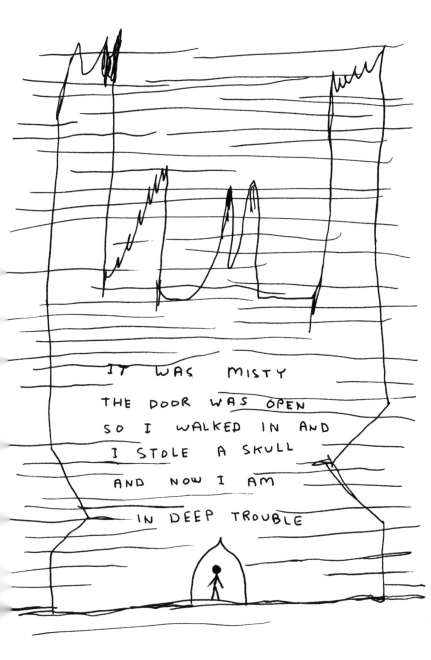

IT WAS MISTY

THE DOOR WAS OPEN

SO I WALKED IN AND

I STOLE A SKULL

AND NOW I AM

IN DEEP TROUBLE

EVEN THOUGH SHE IS ENORMOUS
AND TERRIFYING
SHE IS MORE AFRAID OF YOU
THAN YOU ARE OF HER

CALM DOWN

YOU ARE A DANGER TO THE OTHER DANCERS.

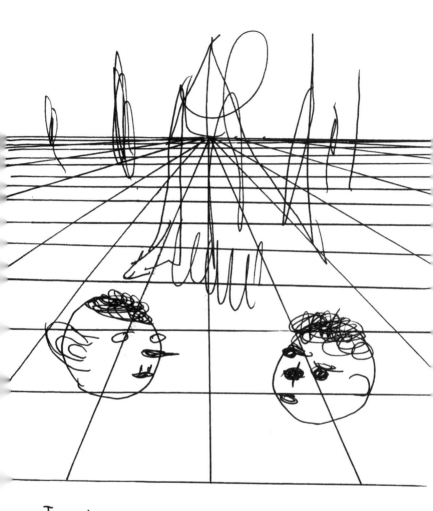

I HAVE GLIMPSED THE
FUTURE

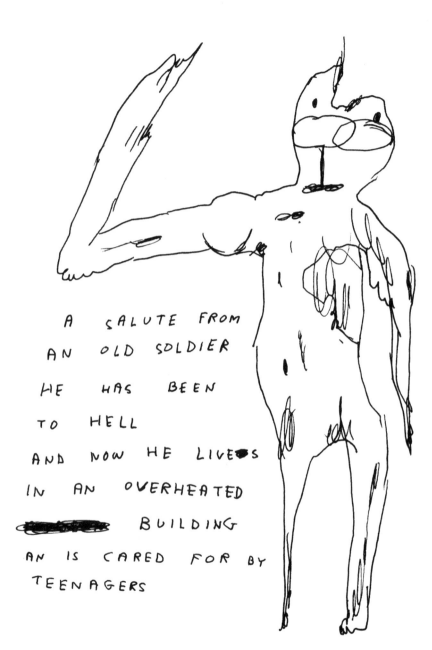

A SALUTE FROM
AN OLD SOLDIER
HE HAS BEEN
TO HELL
AND NOW HE LIVES
IN AN OVERHEATED
~~XXXXXX~~ BUILDING
AN IS CARED FOR BY
TEENAGERS

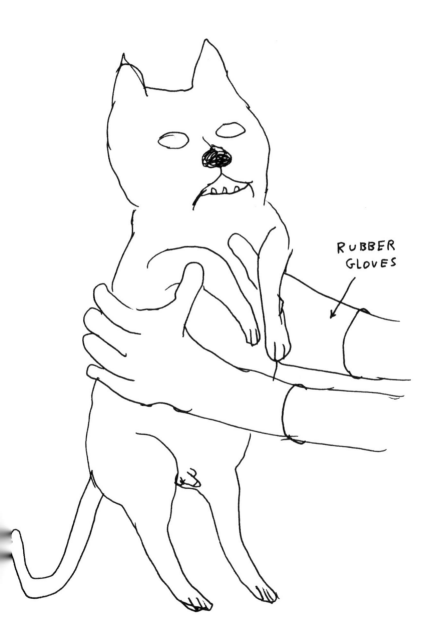

RUBBER
GLOVES

UNTOUCHED

LOOKING OUT OF THE WINDOW

IT IS COLD HERE

BUT THE SPORT IS GREAT

IT IS DEPRESSING ● HOWEVER,
BECAUSE EVERY DAY WE SEE
EVIDENCE THAT THE WORLD
IS DYING.

BOMBS

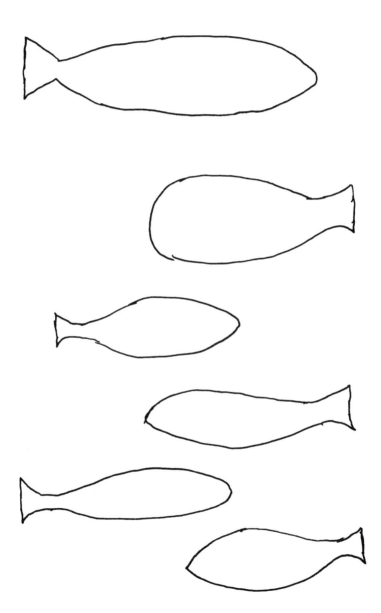

THE SAME

WE'RE ALL THE SAME
ALL OF US EVERYWHERE
IT MIGHT AS WELL BE YOU
WRITING THIS

THE SEQUENCE

I'M GOING TO DRAW A PICTURE
AND THEN I WANT YOU TO LOOK
AT IT
AND THEN ~~COPY~~ IT ~~~~
THEN I WANT YOU TO SHOW IT
TO THAT IDIOT OVER THERE
AND MAKE HIM COPY IT
AND THEN WE'LL MAKE A
RECORDING OF US BEATING HIM UP
AND WE'LL MAKE A C.D.
AND WE'LL USE WHAT HE
DREW FOR THE COVER

I LOVE THE FLAME
I MUST BE NEAR THE FLAME

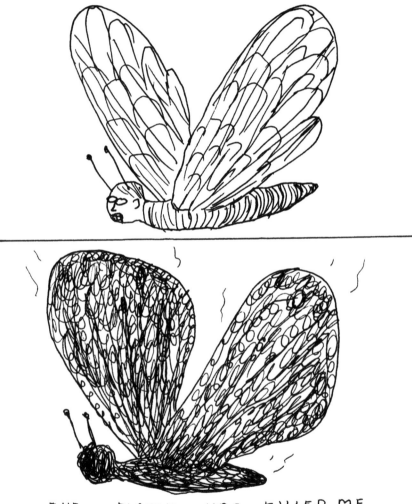

THE FLAME HAS KILLED ME
BUT I LOVED THE FLAME UNTIL THE
MOMENT, IT WAS SWEET ECSTASY

I AM TAKING TAKING HIS HAT
BECAUSE HE DOESN'T NEED IT

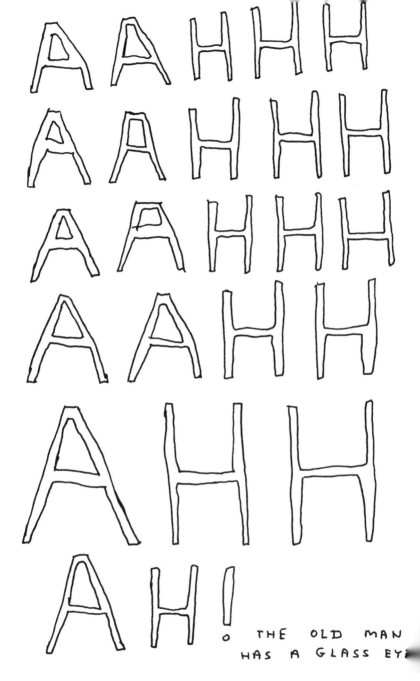

AAHHHH
AAHHHH
AAHHHH
AAHHH
AHHH
AH!

o THE OLD MAN
HAS A GLASS EY

I DO NOT RECOGNIZE THE
AUTHORITY OF THIS COURT

THE MIRROR

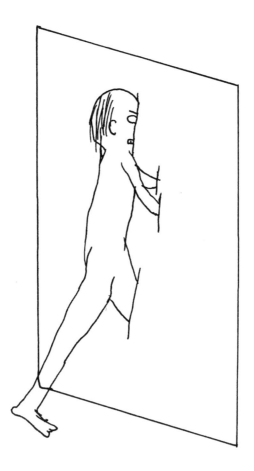

IN I GO

AGAIN

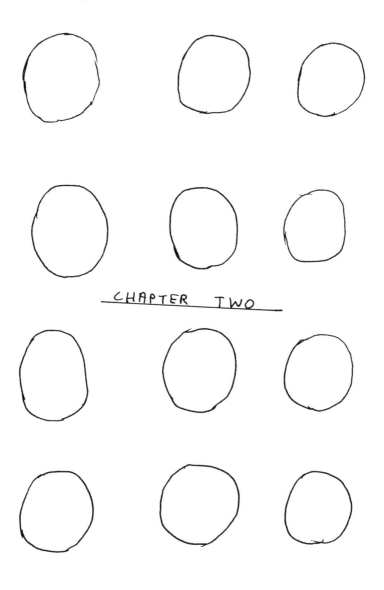

CHAPTER TWO

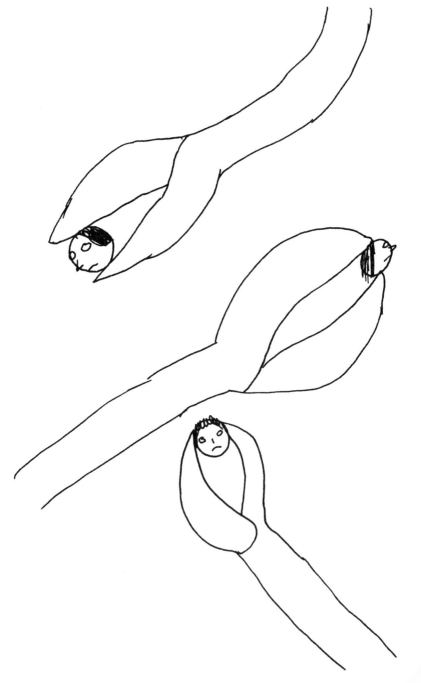

SPEAK UP!
I CAN'T HEAR YOU
YOU   ARE   MUMBLING
YOU   ARE   WHISPERING
YOU   ARE   GETTING SMALLER
■ YOU   ARE   SHRINKING
YOU   ARE   TOO SMALL
YOU   ARE   NOT A PERSON ANYMORE
I CAN'T   SEE YOU
OUR CONVERSATION   IS   OVER

NO MORE GLUE

NOW EVERYTHING WILL FALL APART

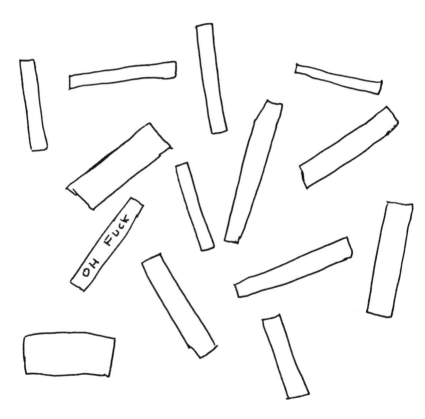

OH FUCK

SPIDERS HANGING FROM YOUR EYES
YOU HAVE VERY LOW STANDARDS
YOUR LOOK IS BEFITTING OF A
BEGGAR
YOU ARE NOT ALLOWED IN THE
RESTAURANT

YOU MUST 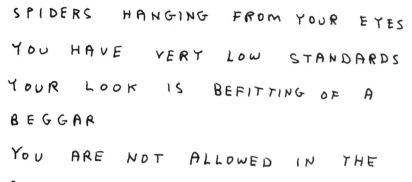 EAT IN THE BAR AREA

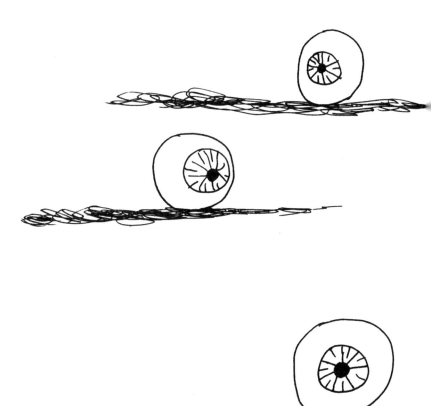

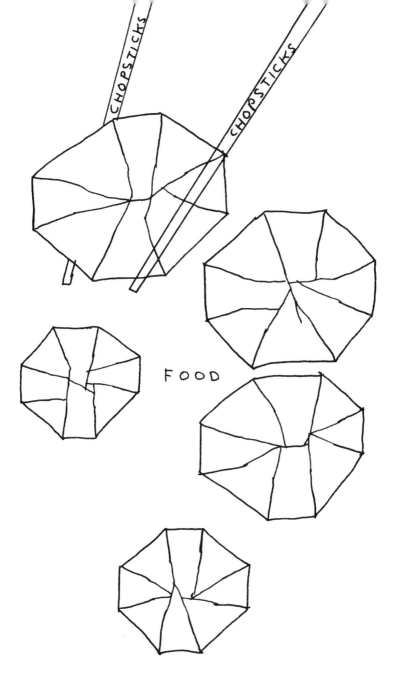

THE FOUR HORSEMEN

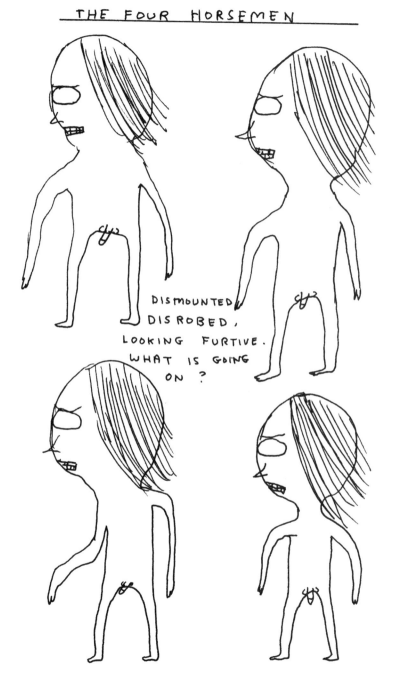

DISMOUNTED,
DISROBED,
LOOKING FURTIVE.
WHAT IS GOING
ON ?

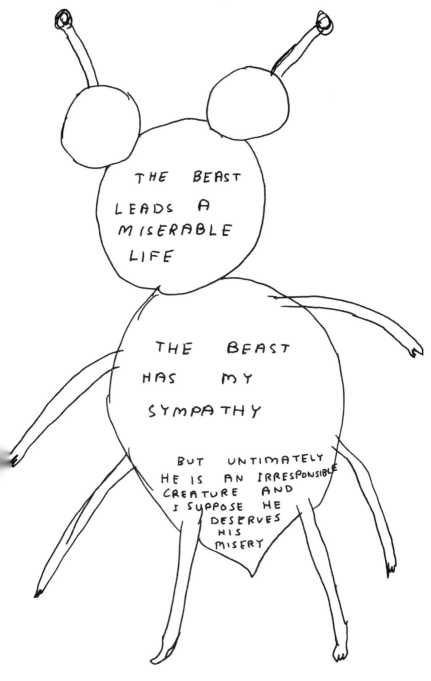

THE BEAST
LEADS A
MISERABLE
LIFE

THE BEAST
HAS MY
SYMPATHY

BUT UNTIMATELY
HE IS AN IRRESPONSIBLE
CREATURE AND
I SUPPOSE HE
DESERVES
HIS
MISERY

BALLOON

THERE   WAS   TOO   MUCH
AIR   IN   IT
MUM   SAID

I SHOULD BE WORKING

I SHOULD BE WORKING
I SHOULDN'T BE HERE DOING THIS
I SHOULD BE SITTING AT MY DESK
IN MY OFFICE
MAKING TELEPHONE CALLS
AND ORDERING DATA

PERHAPS I SHOULD DESTROY THIS
WHEN I HAVE FINISHED
AS IT IS EVIDENCE
OF MY IDLENESS

- - - - - - - - - - - - - - - - - - - -

MUSIC

NO MUSIC HERE
THAT IS THE RULE
NO SINGING OR HUMMING
~~THESE~~ SINGING AND HUMMING
~~THINGS~~ COUNTS AS MUSIC ~~████~~
AND NO TAPPING OF FEET
OR DRUMMING OF FINGERS
THE RULE COVERS THESE THINGS AS WELL ~~████~~
~~█~~ SHOUTING IS ALLOWED
AS LONG AS IT IS NOT RHYTHMIC
TALKING IS ALLOWED
BUT THERE IS A THIN LINE
BETWEEN TALKING AND SINGING
AND IT MUST NOT BE CROSSED

DEAR MR FLY

IT IS TIME FOR YOU TO DIE

~~XXXXXX~~

YOUR ANGRY BUZZING

HAS GOT THE BETTER OF ME

AND I MUST KILL YOU

TO PROTECT MY SANITY

IF I DO NOT KILL YOU

I MAY HAVE TO KILL ONE OF

THE LARGER ~~XXXXXX~~ CREATURES

WHO ARE PLAYING IN THE STREET

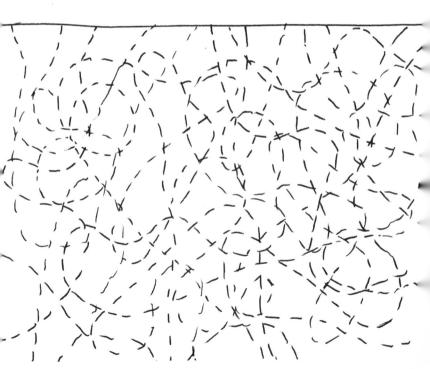

BEER

LEMONADE

THE JOYOUS FEELING
IN MY HEART

IS AKIN TO THE FEELING
I GET WHEN
I SEE AN OLD FRIEND

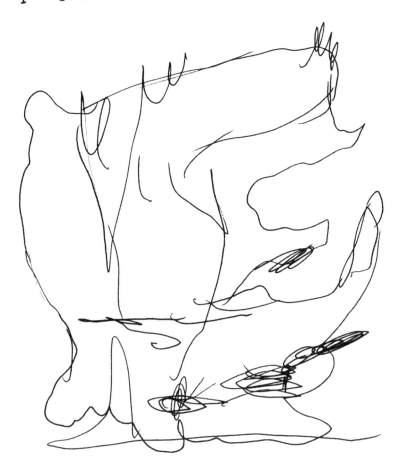

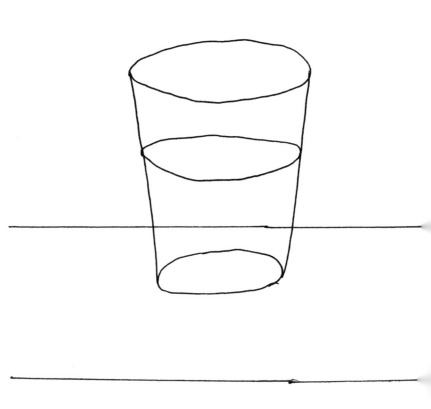

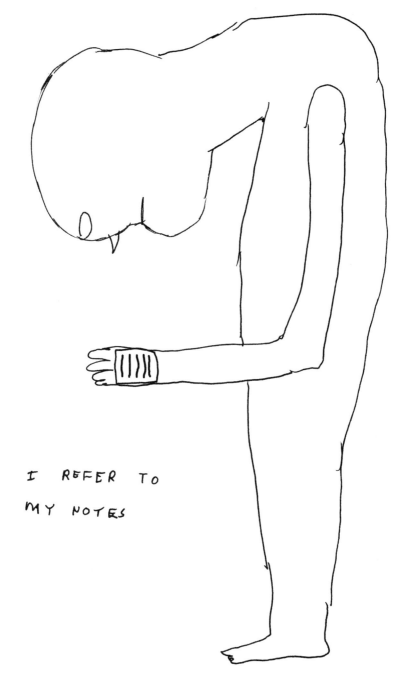

I REFER TO

MY NOTES

SCENES FLASH PAST
AT HIGH SPEED

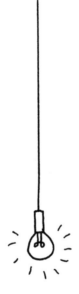

THE LIGHT

THE DARKNESS

SIT DOWN PLEASE
I DO NOT LIKE YOU STANDING
TOWERING O'ER ME

STAND UP NOW PLEASE
IT IS TIME FOR YOU TO GO
GET OUT
YOU HUGE BRUTE

THE STEAM RISES
THE THING IS HOT
THE STEAM DISPERSES
THE THING HAS COOLED
THE PEOPLE LISTEN
THE THING IS TALKING
THE PEOPLE DISPERSE
THE THING IS DRUNK

- - - - - - - - - - - - - - - - - -

EQUATOR

SOUTHERN HEMISPHERE

EVERYTHING MUST HAVE A NAME
EVERYONE MUST PLAY THE GAME
EVERYEAWHERE MUST BE THE SAME

KNOCK DOWN ALL THE BUILDINGS
AND ERECT TENTS ON THE RUBBLE
AND WAIT FOR THE HELICOPTERS
TO DROP PARCELS OF FOOD

CAMERA OVER MY SHOULDER
FILMING EVERYTHING I DO

THE

MAGIC

TREE

AND THEY
WILL KNOW
IT IS THE
MAGIC TREE
BY THE MAGIC
IT DOES

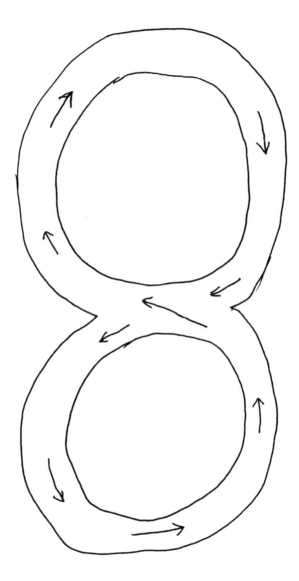

A LIGHT ON IN THE CASTLE
ONE MAN LIVING ALONE IN THE CASTLE
SITTING IN A ROOM
AT A DESK
WRITING A POEM

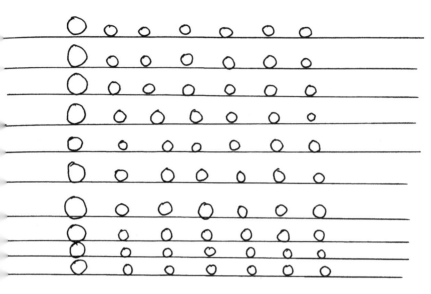

ARROW
POINTING DOWN

PIZZA

ARROW

POINTING UP

THE HOTEL IS FULL
OF TOURISTS
AND BUSINESSMEN
AND PROSTITUTES
THE RESTAURANT IS FULL
OF TOURISTS
AND BUSINESSMEN
AND PROSTITUTES
THE SHOPPING MALL IS FULL
OF TOURISTS
THE JAIL IS FULL
OF TOURISTS
AND PROSTITUTES
THE TRAIN STATION IS FULL
OF TOURISTS
AND BUSINESSMEN
AND PROSTITUTES
THE CINEMA IS CLOSED

ORDINARILY

I WOULD NOT SAY THIS KIND OF THING

BUT TODAY

IS DIFFERENT
TODAY
I FEEL COMPELLED

SUMMON THE DEMON
BRING HIM HERE
I WANT HIM WHERE
I CAN SEE HIM

I'M A ROBOT
I WILL DO WHATEVER YOU ASK
EXCEPT JUGGLE
I CANNOT JUGGLE

ADAM AND THE ANTS
I ATTACKED THEM AND MADE THEM DIE
NOT ADAM, JUST THE ANTS

AND THE MEN IN SUITS
THEY PLAY THIER FLUTES
THEY PLAY THIER STUPID FLUTES

THE ROLLING STONES
I SET ABOUT THEM WITH A HAMMER
AND I BROKE THEM INTO RUBBLE
EXCEPT KEITH RICHARDS
I COULD NOT BREAK HIM
I DID NOT EVEN TRY

AND THE MEN IN SUITS
THEY PLAY THIER FLUTES
THEY PLAY THIER STUPID FLUTES

DURAN DURAN
I RAN THEM OVER IN MY VAN
ALL FIVE OF THEM
THE ORIGINAL LINE UP

AND THE MEN IN SUITS
THEY PLAY THIER FLUTES
THEY PLAY THIER STUPID FLUTES

LORD OF BIG WHEEL
WILL NOT LET OTHERS
RIDE IT
AFTER HIS DEATH
HIS SON WILL TAKE
CONTROL

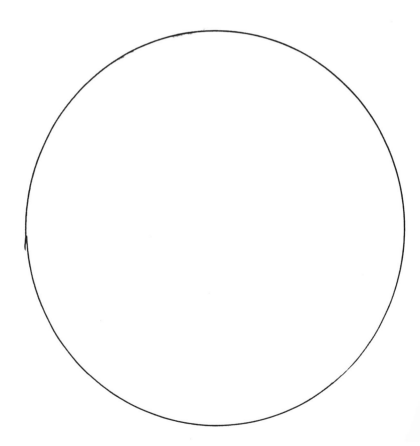

I AM OPEN TO SUGGESTION

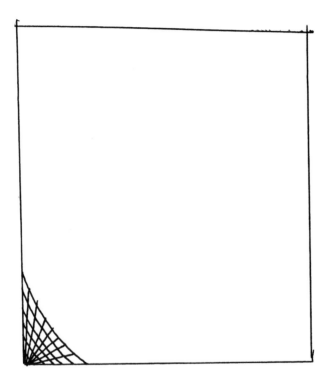

WHAT WILL YOU DO
WHEN ~~⬤~~ THE NIGHT COMES?
WILL YOU GO TO SLEEP?
OR WILL YOU COME WITH ME?
~~█████~~ IN THE WOODS ~~⬤~~
TO LOOK FOR MY SHOE
THAT I ~~████~~ LOST
EARLIER TODAY
WHILST BEING CHASED
BY A MAN WITH AN AXE

SWITCHES

OFF AND ON
UP AND DOWN
~~OPEN~~ OPEN AND CLOSED
LOCKED AND UNLOCKED
ALIVE AND DEAD
QUIET AND LOUD
FAST AND SLOW
VERY FAST AND STOP
SLOW AND STOP
SILENT AND DEAFING
LOCKED AND LOCKED
UNLOCKED AND UNLOCKED
OFF AND OFF
ON AND ON
UP AND UP
DOWN AND DOWN
FORWARDS AND BACKWARDS
FORWARDS AND NOT FORWARDS
BACKWARDS AND DEAD

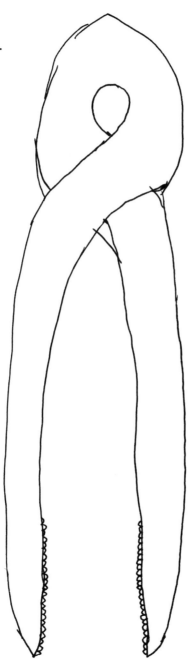

THE DRONE

I'M FED UP
WITH THE CONSTANT DRONING
I WISH I COULD SWITCH A SWITCH
AND MAKE IT STOP
IT MAKES IT HARD TO CONCENTRATE
I AM TRYING TO READ A BOOK
ABOUT THE NAZIS

GIVE THE DOG A BONE
GIVE THE HORSE SOME HAY
GIVE THE ELEPHANT A PEANUT
GIVE THE HEDGEHOG SOME MILK
PUT FUEL IN THE CAR
GIVE THE APE A BANANA
WIND UP THE CLOCK

CAN YOU CATCH HEAVY OBJECTS
FALLING FROM THE SKY?

CAN YOU LEAP OVER STREAMS?
DO YOU FIND SUCH THINGS EASY?
DO YOU WANNA DANCE?
DO ~~DO~~ YA DO ~~DO~~ YA DO YA
DO YA WANNA DANCE?
OR WOULD YOU PREFER
TO GO FOR A WALK?
ARE YOU ABLE
TO FIX THE LIGHTS
IN MY HOUSE?
EVERYTHING
~~xxxxxx~~
HAS GONE

DARK

AN ADVERT IN A NEWSPAPER

WOULD YOU RUN WITH ME
THROUGH A FIELD OF MUCK?
WOULD YOU HELP ME DIG A HOLE?
WOULD YOU COME DOWN THE HOLE
WITH ME?
WOULD YOU HELP ME
GET THE STUFF OUT OF THE HOLE
WOULD YOU HELP ME
SELL THE STUFF?
WOULD YOU HELP ME
RE-BURY THE STUFF WE COULDN'T SELL?

— — — — — — — — — — — — — — — — — —

FURIOUS

I'M FURIOUS

FLUFF
CAUGHT BY THE WIND
BLOWN TO OTHER COUNTRIES
WHERE IT COLLECTS
AND IS GATHERED
BY PEASANTS
WHO MAKE THINGS WITH IT
TO SELL TO TOURISTS

BIRD
FLYING LOW
IN A SKY FILLED WITH FLUFF
FLUFF IN ITS EYES
IT COLLIDES WITH A CHIMNEY

ARM
OF THE BANDIT
PULL IT
AND SEE WHAT YOU GET
SKULL
SKULL
SKULL
YOU WIN A HOLIDAY

THE NEST

THE NEST IS MADE FROM CLOTHES
SOME DIRTY SOME CLEAN
THERE IS ALSO A DUVET
AND PILLOWS
AND A BLANKET
THERE ARE MAGAZINES
AND A BOOK BELONGING TO ME
AND SOME C.D.s
WITHOUT CASES
THERE IS A SHOE
AND A HAT
AND A PIECE OF TOAST
THERE IS MAKE-UP
AND ~~SOME~~ COTTON WOOL
THERE MAY BE SOME KEYS
BUT THEY CANNOT BE FOUND
THERE MAY BE AN MP3 PLAYER
~~BUT~~ ~~PERHAPS~~ IN THERE ALSO
THE~~ME~~ BIRD IS NOT IN THE NEST
SHE HAS GONE TO THE SUPERMARKET

DO NOT TELL ME OF YOUR TROUBLES

IT MAKES ME SLEEPY

WISH GRAVY

- MAKE ME SOME WISH GRAVY
- HOW IS IT MADE ?
- HOW DO YOU THINK IT IS MADE ?
- IS IT MADE FROM WISHES ?
- YES
- AND ANYTHING ELSE ?
- HOT WATER AND CORNFLOUR
- IS IT MADE THE SAME AS NORMAL GRAVY ?
- YES
- SHALL I ADD BEEF STOCK ?
- GOOD HEAVENS NO !
- WHY ?
- BECAUSE THAT WOULD SPOIL IT

BLACK HAT

MAN IN BLACK HAT
APPEARS FROM NOWHERE
HE ~~PUTS~~ PUTS A SIGN
ON THE WALL
IT SAYS :

MAGIC SHOW
THIS SUNDAY
VENUE T.B.C.
8 PM

THEN HE DISAPPEARS

EAT POISONOUS BERRIES
JUMP OFF CLIFF
DROWN IN RIVER

CHAPTER THREE
(THE FINAL CHAPTER)

WHO WILL PLAY THE GOAT?
NO ONE WILL PLAY THE GOAT?
SOMEONE MUST PLAY THE PART
OF THE GOAT OR THE STORY
WILL MAKE NO SENSE.
WE CAN'T USE A ~~●~~ REAL GOAT

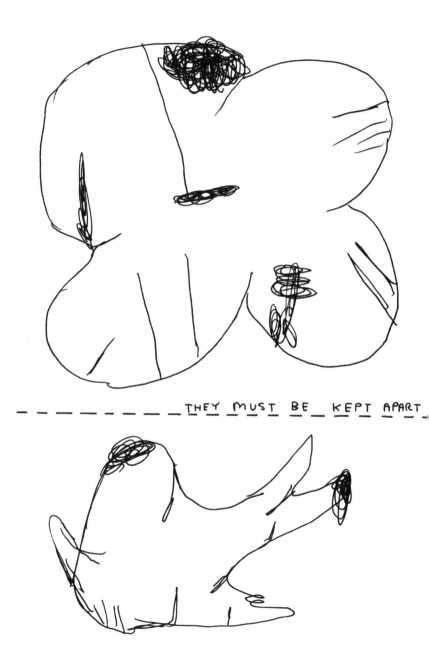

THEY MUST BE KEPT APART

THE SKY

THE SKY WAS NOT MEANT FOR US

IT WAS MEANT FOR  BIRDS

AND WASPS

AND FLIES

AND BALLOONS

AND CLOUDS

AND SMOKE

AND STARS

AND UN-MANNED SURVIELLANCE AIRCRAFT

THE SONG

THEY SANG A SONG
WE LISTENED TO THE SONG
WE WROTE DOWN THE WORDS
OF THE SONG
WE TRIED TO LEARN THE SONG
BUT WE COULD NOT ⬛
REMEMBER IT
WE HAD TO KEEP LOOKING AT
WHAT WE HAD WRITTEN DOWN
THIS MADE PEOPLE ANGRY
"EVERYONE KNOWS THE SONG"
THEY SAID
"YOU SHOULD HAVE LEARNED THE
SONG BY NOW"
THEY SAID
"EVEN CHILDREN KNOW THE SONG
BY HEART"
BUT WE DID NOT KNOW THE SONG
BY HEART
AND NO MATTER HOW WE TRIED
WE COULD NOT LEARN IT
SO ⬛ EVERYONE IN SOCIETY
STOPPED SPEAKING TO US
AND EVENTUALLY
WE WERE PUT IN PRISON

YOU FEATURE IN MY DREAMS
I HAVE SEX WITH YOU
THEN I KILL YOU
THEN I HAVE SEX WITH YOU AGAIN
THEN YOU COME BACK TO LIFE
THEN I KILL YOU AGAIN
THEN I HAVE SEX WITH YOU AGAIN
THEN I EAT YOU
THEN YOU COME BACK TO LIFE
AND YOU COME OUT OF MY BOTTOM
THEN I KILL YOU AGAIN

EYES   SHUT

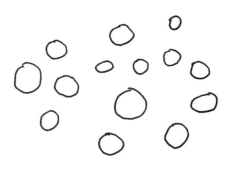

EYES   OPEN

PRISON

WALLS

BABIES

BABIES WITH BEARDS
BABIES THAT SPEAK WITH ADULT
VOICES
BABIES RIDING HORSES
BABIES DRIVING CARS
BABIES AS JAILORS
ADULTS IN PRISON
BABIES SMOKING CIGARETTES
BABIES GETTING MARRIED
BABIES HAVING BABIES
BABIES GETTING OLD
WITH GREY HAIR
OLD BABIES

GOD MAKES THE FLOWERS GROW
THEY GROW IN SHIT
AND HAVE SEX WITH INSECTS
AND ARE PICKED AND GIVEN TO WHORE

WE MUST NOT
QUESTION GOD'S WAY

WE MUST
JUST ACCEPT
IT.

GNOME IS
AMAZED BY YOU

GNOME WILL
TELL OTHER GNOMES

GNOMES WILL COME
TO GAWP AT YOU

YOUR ORATORY
WILL BE ADVERSELY
AFFECTED

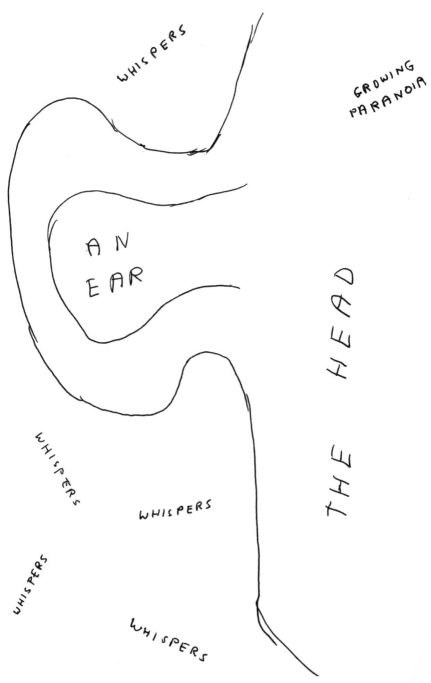

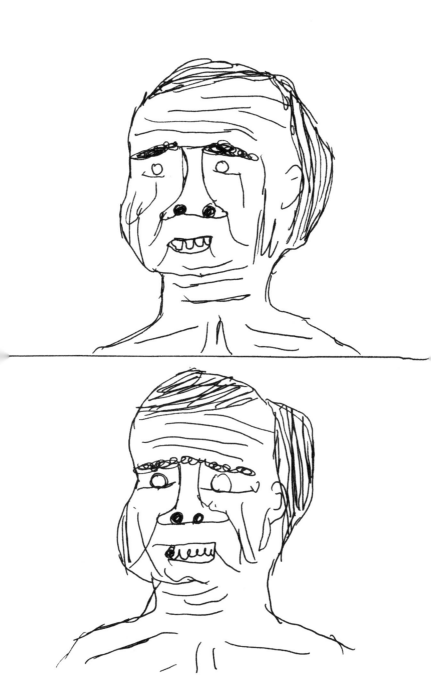

- DID YOU ENJOY YOUR TIME AWAY?
- I HAVEN'T BEEN AWAY

- REALLY ?
- YES, I HAVE BEEN HERE ALL THE
  TIME
- REALLY ?
- YES. IT IS YOU WHO HAVE BEEN
  AWAY. I HAVE BEEN HERE ALONE,
  COUNTING THE HOURS UNTIL YOUR
  RETURN
- REALLY ?

- YES

UNDERSTAND THIS:

ALL FOUR
OF US
WERE NAKED
WE HAD TO
CLIMB A
~~LADDE~~ LADDE

LOOK AT THE
BONE

DO NOT LICK THE
BONE

DO NOT PUT THE
BONE IN YOUR
MOUTH

THE BONE IS TO
BE USED AS
EVIDENCE

AND IT WILL
RUIN EVERYTHING
IF YOU START
CHEWING ON IT

THE SPIDERS ARE COMING TO TOWN
THEY HAVE BEEN KICKED OUT
OF THIER TOWN
BY THE MAYOR
WHO DOESN'T LIKE SPIDERS
AND THEY ARE COMING TO
OUR TOWN
TO BUILD WEBS
AND HAVE BABIES
AND EAT FLIES

THE PERFECT PLACE

I'M GOING TO CLIMB UP
AND GO IN THAT HOLE
AND I'M GOING TO LAY
MY EGGS IN THERE
AND IT'S GOING TO BE GREAT

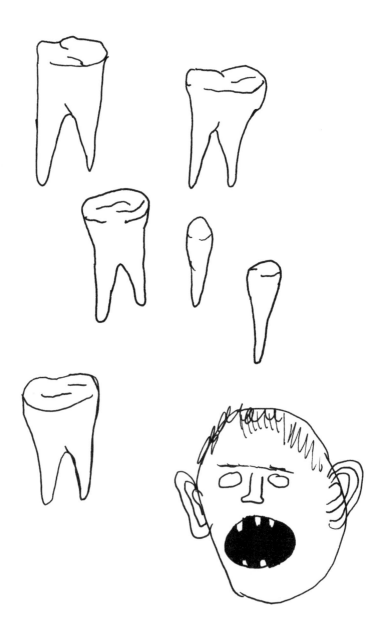

THE BIG GREY RAT

HE WAS LOATHSOME
HE WAS LIKE A BIG GREY RAT
FROM THE SEWER
HE HAD NO BUSINESS
BEING ON TELEVISION
SO I TURNED IT OFF
AND I LOOKED OUT OF THE WINDOW
FOR AN HOUR AND A HALF
AND THEN I WENT TO BED

DURING THE NIGHT
I WOKE UP AND COULD NOT FEEL MY ARM
I HAD BEEN SLEEPING WITH IT
IN AN AWKWARD POSITION
SO I GOT UP
AND WALKED ABOUT
AND SHOOK MY ARM
AND I TURNED ON THE TELEVISION
AND THAT LOATHSOME BASTARD
WAS STILL THERE TALKING
SO I MADE SOME TOAST

GO YOUR OWN WAY

YOU CAN GO YOUR OWN WAY
I DON'T WANT YOU COMING MY WAY
WHY?
BECAUSE MY WAY IS OVER-SUBSCRIBED
THERE ARE NO MORE PLACES
AVAILABLE FOR PEOPLE TO
COME MY WAY
MY WAY HAS BEEN OVER-SUBSCRIBED
FOR QUITE SOME TIME NOW
THERE ARE NO ~~PLACES~~ STAND-BY
PLACES AVAILABLE EITHER
THEY ARE ALL TAKEN
SO YOU CAN'T COME MY WAY
WHY?
BECAUSE THE RATIO OF
FOLLOWERS TO LEADERS
WOULD BE TOO GREAT IF
WE ACCEPTED ANY MORE
AND IT WOULD CONTRAVENE
SAFETY REGULATIONS

Mmmm Mm Mmm mmm

MMM M M Mmm mmm

MMM

WORDS WRITTEN DOWN ON A PAGE

- A CARDBOARD BOX
- WHAT IS IN THE CARDBOARD BOX?
- WHAT DO YOU THINK?
- I DON'T KNOW
- TRY TO IMAGINE
- (IMAGINES) AN EGG
- WHAT IS THE EGG MADE OF?
- I DON'T KNOW
- TRY TO IMAGINE
- (IMAGINES) EGG MATERIAL
- AND WHAT IS INSIDE THE EGG?
- I DON'T KNOW
- TRY TO IMAGINE
- (IMAGINES) SLIME
- AND WHAT DOES THE SLIME TASTE LIKE
- I CAN'T DO THIS ANY MORE
- TRY TO IMAGINE
- NO I CAN'T DO IT. I'VE GOT A HEADACHE

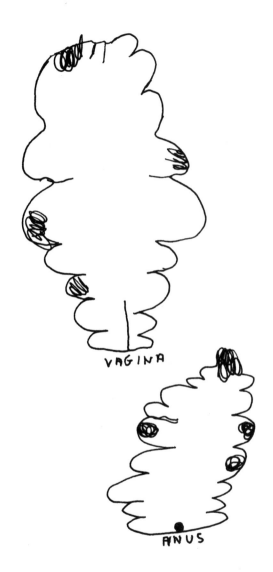

VAGINA

ANUS

TO START WITH
I THOUGHT I WAS UNLUCKY
BUT THEN I REALISED
I WAS ACTUALLY VERY LUCKY

COMPULSIVE EATING

I ATE THE PIZZA

BECAUSE IT WAS THERE

I ATE THE BISCUITS

BECAUSE THEY WERE THERE

I ATTEMPTED TO EAT

THE CARPET

BECAUSE I WAS CURIOUS

IT HAD BEEN THERE

FOR SOME TIME

WORD SEARCH:

ARTHRITIS

NUMBER SEARCH:

8

STOP   YOUR   CRYING
PLEASE   STOP
IT   IS   UNSEEMLY
FOR   A   MASS   MURDERER
TO   BE   SEEN   CRYING

YOU ARE NOT DEAD YET

NO ONE IN
YOUR COFFIN

ALREADY YOU ARE HERE